GRIMORIUM VERUM

Éditions Unicursal Publishers

unicursal.ca

ISBN 978-2-89806-615-3 (Paperback)

ISBN 978-2-89806-616-0 (Hardcover)

First English Edition, Ostara 2024

GRIMORIUM VERUM

or

THE TRUE GRIMOIRE

The Most Approved Keys of
Solomon, the Hebrew Rabbi

Vel probatissimè Salomonis Claviculæ
Rabini Hebraïci in quibus tum naturalia
tum super naturalia secreta licet abditis-
sirna in promptu apparent. Modo operator per nessaria et contenta faciat scia
tamen oportet Demonum potentia dum
taxat per agantur.

Translated from the Hebrew by
PLAINGIÈRE,
Dominican Jesuit.

With a Collection of Rare and
Astounding Magical Secrets.

AT MEMPHIS,
BY ALIBECK, THE ÆGYPTIAN.
1517.

GREAT WHEEL
OR PLANETARY SPHERE
BY JJJ.C.

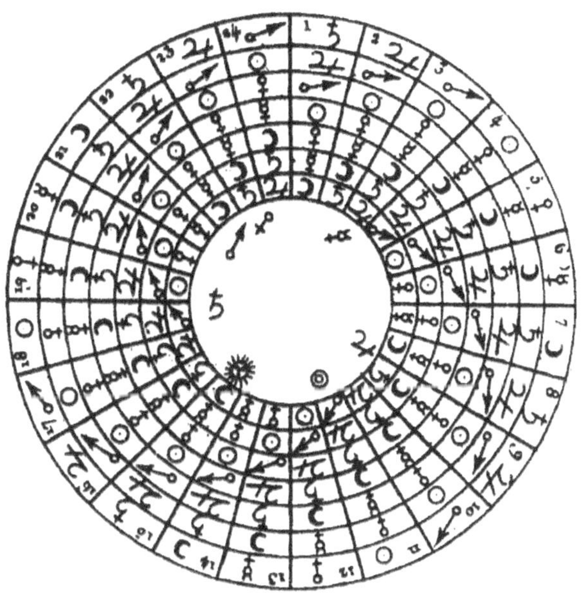

GRIMORIUM VERUM.

HE begins the *Sanctum regum*, says the King of Spirits, or the Clavicles of Solomon, very learn-ed Negromantian, or Rabin, Hebrews.

In the First Part.

Is contained various dispositions of characters, by which the Powers, the Spirits or, rather, the Devils are invoked, to make them come when you please, each according to their power, and to compel them to bring whatever is asked of them, and this without ever being worried, provided also that they are content on their end; for

these kinds of creatures do not give anything for nothing. You will also find in the
first Part the means of calling forth these
Spirits, being Aerial, Terrestrial, Marine,
and Infernal, as you will see and notice in
the ways that will be taught.

In the Second Part.

Are taught the secrets, both Natural
and Supernatural, which operate through
the power of Demons. You will find the
manner to make use of them, and all without deceit.

In the Third Part.

Is the Key to the Work, with the manner of using it. But before moving forth,
you must be instructed of the following
characters.

Here begins the Key to the work.

THERE are three Powers, which are: Lucifer, Beelzebuth and Astaroth. You must engrave the following reversed character in this manner, so that the engraving is made at the appropriate hour. *Videas & facies.*

Crede mihi, nihil præter mittendum est, see and act; believe me, all this is of consequence, nothing is to be forgotten.

You must carry the aforesaid character with you. If you are male, in the right pocket, *qui scribendus est proprio tuo sanguine* [and it is to be written in your own blood], or that of a sea-turtle. You will put at the two half-circles the first letter of your name and surname. And if you wish more, you may engrave this character on an emerald or ruby, for they both have some sympathy for the Spirits, *particulariter cum solaribus qui sunt sapientissimi et per familiare etiam atque etiam meliores aliis* [especially those of the Sun, who are the most knowledgeable, and are better than the others].

If you are a female, carry the character on the left side, between the breasts, like a Reliquary; and always observing, as much as the other sex, to write or have engraved the character on the day and in the hour of Mars.

Fac, obedias spiritibus qui tibi obedient [Obey the Spirits in this, that they may obey thee]. The prelude is explained, where we give in the chapter the explanation of the Spirits, which is very necessary to be read and well noted to have an understanding of this divine work. The Spirits who are powerful and exalted, serve only their confidants and intimate friends, by the pact made or to be made according to certain characters at the will of Singambuth or of his Secretary. *Caveas, lector vel operatort, ne tales Spiritus te in prompt accipiant* [Be careful, reader or operator, that such Spirits do not take you in readiness].

Rabidanadas of which we will give you the intelligence and the perfect knowledge to call, conjure and constrain, as you will see in the Key, where you will be given a method of making a pact with the Spirits who will come according to the character and temperament of the one who wishes to invoke them; it will be very difficult to identify, because... *Sic volo, sic jubeo, sic pro ratione voluntas* [Thus I will, thus I command, thus the will of reason.].

The obscure and difficult thing would be too clear if it were explained, *non dico per me, sed etiam per subjectos, quia illud spectat Rabidinadap, il est, faciendum est jussu illius* [I do not say it through myself, but also through the subjects, because that is what Rabidinadap sees, and it must be done at his command].

However, after you have offered some fine incense, and have watered it *ex proprio tuo cruore, sanguine* [with your own blood], or that of a male kid, *cum invocatione spirituum orientalium* [with the invocation of the Eastern Spirits] in its place.

Ut illud sit hoc in opere inclusum minimo clarum in doctis [That this is included in this work, is the least clear among the learned], it is certain, if you want to make some effort and give it all your care, *hoc in promptis apparebit, il, &c.* [this will appear in due time, etc.]

Of the Nature of Pacts.

THERE are only two kinds of pact, the tacit and the apparent.

You will know each of them, as long as you take care to read this little book. Know, however, that there are many kinds of Spirits, some engaging and others not engaging, *sive minime.*

Those who engage, it is when you give the Spirit with whom you make a pact, something which belongs to you, that is what we must be careful about, *quia amicus fiet capitalis, fiet inimicus* [because a friend will become a chief, lest he becomes an enemy.].

In regard to Spirits, *superiores et secundi inferiores* [there are superiors and inferiors].

Titulus superiores sunt [The names of the superiors are]: Lucifer, Beelzebuth, Astaroth. *Imperator principit comes. Tres Spiritus omnia possunt*[1]. [The emperor comes first. The three Spirits can accomplish anything.]

The inferiors of Lucifer *sunt incolæ Europæ & Asiæ, qui obediunt* [are in Europe and Asia, and obey him. Beelzebuth *habitant Affricam, qui capiunt leges* [lives in Africa], and Astaroth inhabits America. Of these, each of them has two who order their subjects all that which the Emperor has resolved to do in all the world, *& vice versâ jubent quæ sunt facienda* [and vice versa they command what must be done.].

---

1 *Caveas tamen ne pavescant.* [However, be careful not to feed them.]

CHARACTERS
OF LUCIFER

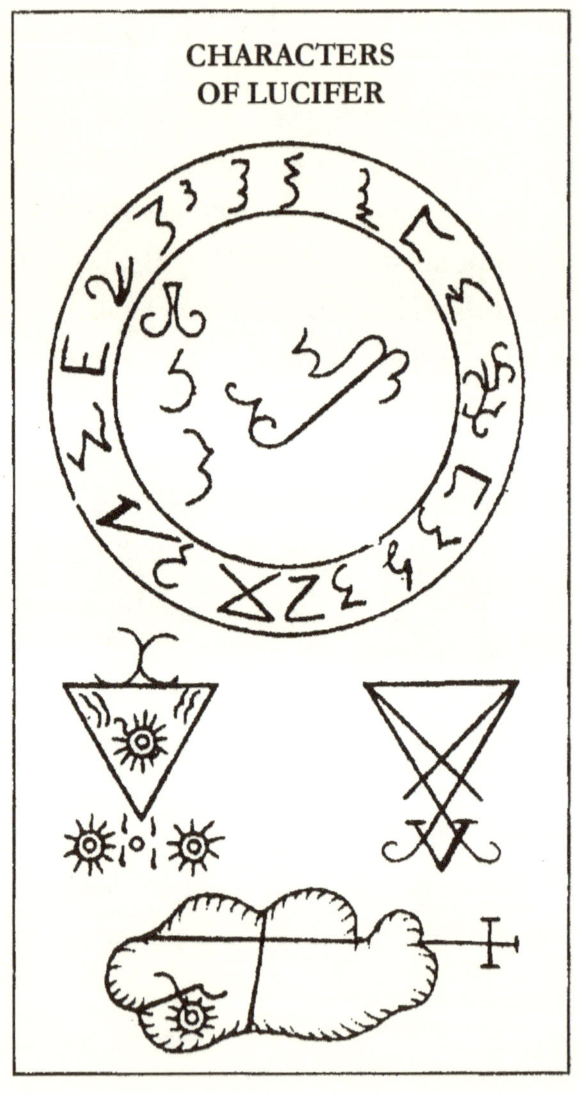

CHARACTERS
OF BELZEBUTH

CHARACTERS
OF ASTAROTH

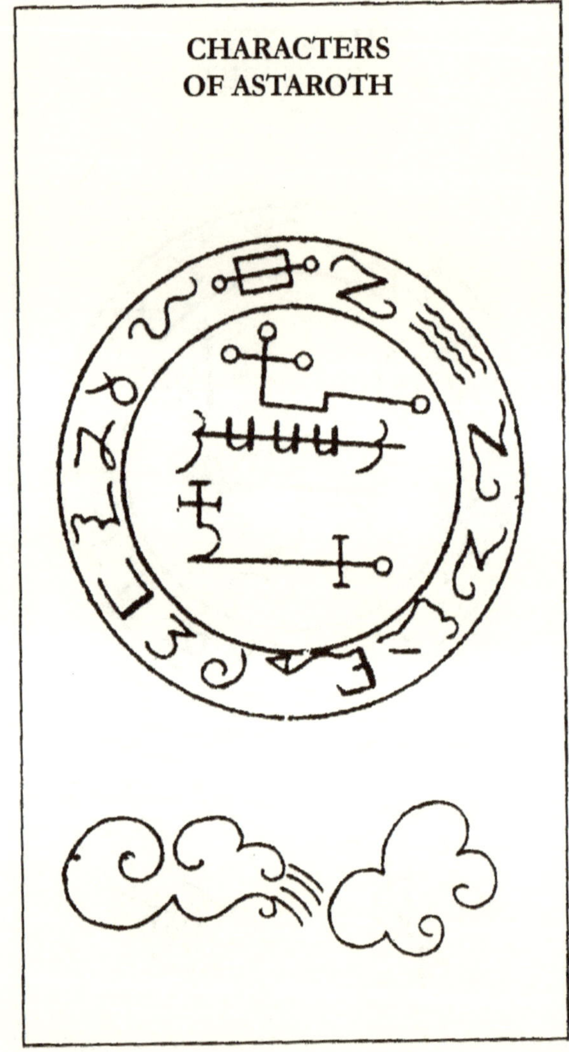

Spirits do not always appear under the same forms, it is because they are not themselves of matter, *ab omni materia;* it is therefore necessary that they borrow a body to appear to us; thus they can take the form and figure as they see fit.

Lucifer appears *sub forma et figura pulcherrima pueri. Quando irascitur, rubicundus apparet* [under the most beautiful shape and form of a child. When he is angry, he appears to be red]. Although, there is nothing monstrous about him.

Beelzebuth sometimes appears in monstrous forms, sometimes like a monstrous calf, at times like a goat, with a long tail. *Attamen sæpissime apparet sub figura muscæ* [However, he most often appears under the form of a fly] of an extreme size. *Quando irascitur, vomit fluminas et hurle sicut lupus.* [When he is angry, he vomits fire and screams like a wolf].

Astaroth apparet colore nigro et candido sub figura humana sæpissimè et aliquandò sub figura asini [Astaroth appears in black and white colour, under a human form and some-what under the figure of a donkey].

Here are the three characters of Lucifer below his circle.

The following are those of Beelzebuth and Astaroth placed below their own circles.

It is only necessary, when you desire to invoke them, to call them by their characters, which they themselves have given. When you wish to invoke and obtain something from them, in the manner taught in the Third Part, *alitem frustrà laborares* [or you would labour in vain].

Let us descend to the Inferiors, *inferiores*. Two of Lucifer, Put Satanakia and Agalierap. Those of Beelzebuth are Tarchimache and Fleruty, their characters are such.

The two inferiors of Astaroth are Sagatana and Nesbiros. These are their characters.

There are yet other Demons apart from these, who are under the Duke Syrach.

There are eighteen of them, and their names are:

1. Clauneck
2. Musisin
3. Bechaud
4. Frimost
5. Klepoth
6. Khil
7. Mersilde
8. Clisthert
9. Sirchacle

10. Segal
11. Hicpacth
12. Humots
13. Frucissière
14. Guland
15. Surgat
16. Morail
17. Frutimière
18. Huictiigaras

Here are their characters.

Put Satanakia

Agalierap

Fleruty

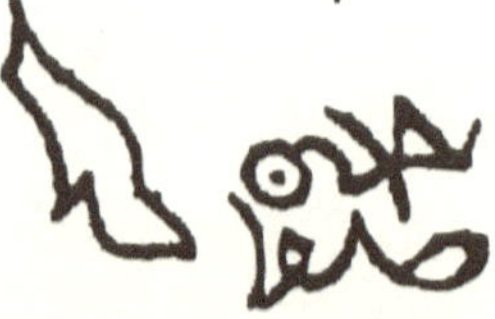

Sagatana

Nesbiros

6.   *Khil.*

7.   *Merfide.*

8.   *Chstheret.*

9.   *Sirchade.*

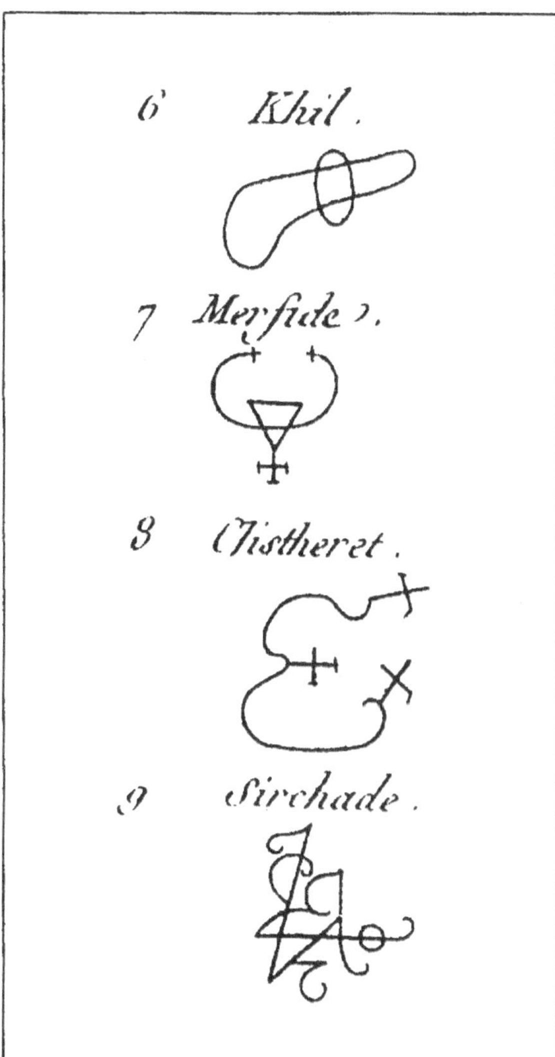

10   SEGAL

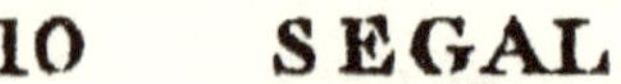

11   HIEPÀCTH

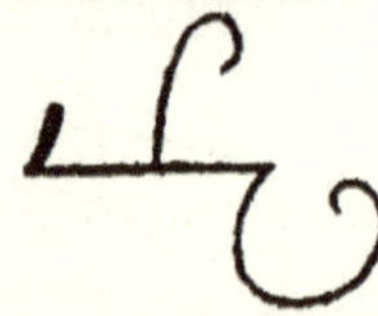

12   HUMOTS

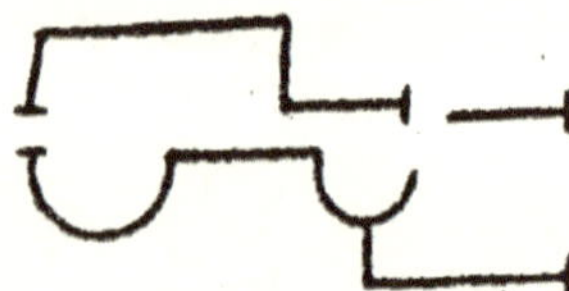

13   FRUCISSIERE

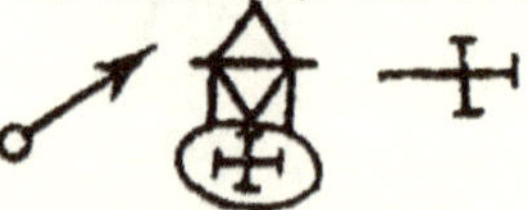

14   GULAND

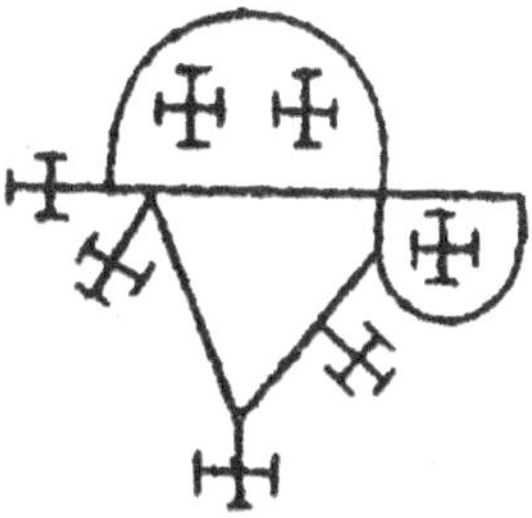

15   SURGAT

16   MORAIL

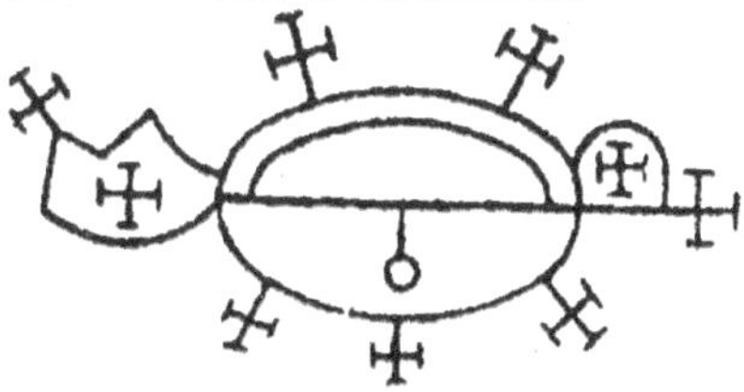

17 *Frutimiere.*

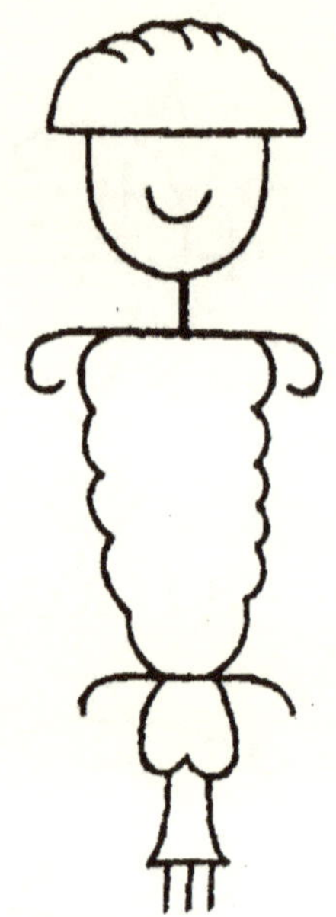

18 *Huctugaras*

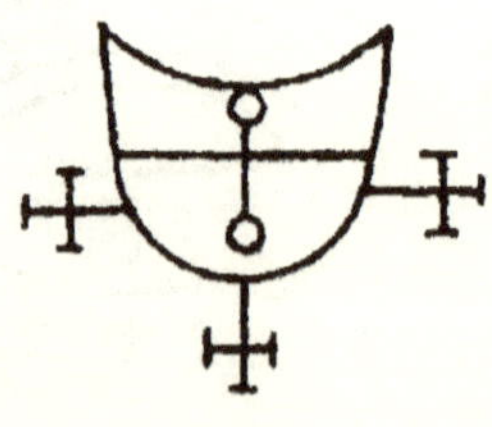

Second Part of the S. S. J.

Agla * Adonay * Jehova *

THERE are still other Demons; but as they have no power, we shall not speak of them. The powers of the eighteen above-mentioned are such:

Clauneck has power over goods and riches; he can cause treasures to be found to whom makes a pact with him; he can give great riches, for he is much loved by Lucifer. It is he who causes money to be brought, *obedias illi, & obediet.*

Musisin has power over great Lords, he teaches all that happens in the Republics, and the affairs of the Allies.

Bechaud has power in winds and storms, in lightning, hail and rain; either with toads and other things of this nature.

Frimost has power over women and girls, and makes you enjoy them.

Klepoth makes you see all sorts of dances.

Khil makes and causes great earth-quakes.

Merfilde has the power to transport anyone in an instant, anywhere we wish.

Clisthert allows you to have day or night, when you desire.

Sirchade has the power to make you see all sorts of animals of any kind that they may be.

Segal shows all kinds of wonders and chimeras, both natural and supernatural.

Hicpacth will bring you a faraway person in an instant.

Humots has the power to bring you any book that will make you pleased.

Frucissiere resurrect the dead.

Guland has the power to excite and cause all kinds of illnesses.

Surgat opens every kind of lock.

Morail has the power to make anything invisible.

Frutimiere prepares all kinds of feasts for you.

Huictiigara excites everyone to sleep and wakefulness, and other strong unwelcome insomnia.

Under Satanachia and Saticiæ, there are forty-five Demons, and according to some others, fifty-four, under the power of which there are four, two major ones, and the others are of no great consequence; the four are such:

1. Sergutthy.
2. Heramael.
3. Trimasel.
4. Sustugriel.

These Spirits are very necessary, for what is happening; because they act easily and promptly, provided they are pleased with the operator, that is to say, of him who wishes to obtain something from them.

Of their Powers.

1. Sergutthy has power over maidens and wives, as long as the occasion is favourable.

2. Heramael teaches the art of medicine, gives complete knowledge of any illness and its complete cure, makes known all plants, the place, where they are to be found, and when to gather them, their virtues and their composition in the making a complete cure.

3. Trimasel teaches chemistry and all the tricks, and gives the real secret of making the powder of projection, which has the power to change imperfect metals, such as lead, iron, tin and copper, quicksilver into true good silver and gold, into true Sun or Moon, according to his oath, etc. *Modò sit contentus operatoris & vice versâ.*

4. Sustugriel teaches the art of magic, and gives familiar Spirits that can be used for all purposes, and he also gives Mandragores.

Under both Agalierapts and Tarihimal is Elelogap, who has power over the waters. His character is thus.

Under Nebirots are both Hael and Sergulath.

Hael teaches to write all kinds of letters, and immediately makes people speak in all kinds of languages, and gives explanations of the most hidden things. Sergulath provides all kinds of speculations, and teaches the wiles of war, and the means of breaking enemies. Their characters are as follows.

There are still other subordinates who depend of Hael and Sergulath, who have much power, they are eight in number.

1. Proculo.	5. Aglasis.
2. Haristum.	6. Sidragosum.
3. Brulefer	7. Minosons.
4. Pentagnony.	8. Bucon.

Here are their characters.

Minosons. 7.

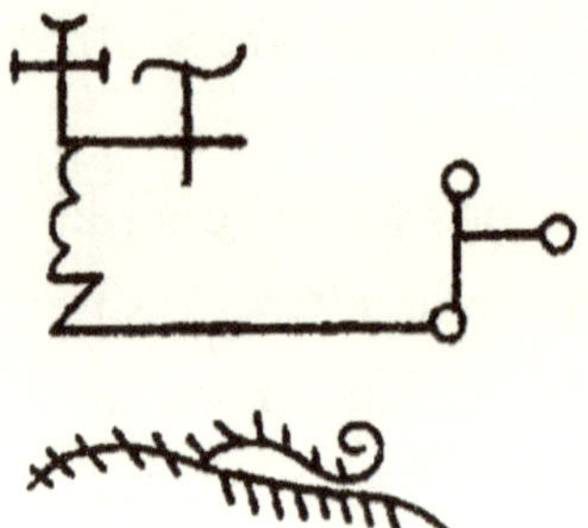

Bucons. 8.

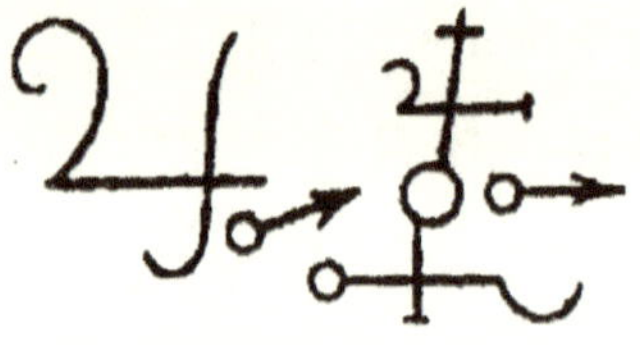

Klepoth 5.

Of their Powers.

1. Proculo, excite to sleep for forty-eight hours, and gives knowledge of the Realms of sleep, etc.

2. Haristum has the power to cause anyone to pass through fire without being burned.

3. Brulefer makes you to be beloved of women.

4. Pentagnony has the power to make you invisible, and to make you loved by great Lords.

5. Aglasis can carry anyone anywhere in the world.

6. Sidragosum causes any girl to dance in the nude.

7. Minoson makes anyone win at any games.

8. Bucon has the power to put hatred and jealousy between one sex and the other.

Enough has been said about the Spirits; we shall give the conjurations and the way of summoning them in this part which follows.

It is necessary to observe very carefully not to forget anything about their characters, and of the time that will be marked.

Third part of S. S.

Invocation.

Heloy † Tau † Varaf † Panthon † Homnorcum † Elemiah † Serugeath † Agla † On † Tetragrammaton † Casily †.

This invocation must be made on virgin parchment, with the character that is made by Scyrlin, of whom it is spoken in the First Book; because on him all the others depend, as a messenger of the others, and who can compel them to come and appear in spite of themselves, for he has the power of the Emperor.

Orison. Preparation.

Lord God Adonay, who hast made man in Thine own image and resemblance; and I, unworthy sinner as I am, beseech Thee to deign bless † and sanctify this water, so that it may be salutary to my body and my soul, and let all deception come out of me. Lord God, all-powerful and ineffable, and who led Thy people out of the land of Ægypt, and has enabled them to cross the Red Sea with dry feet, grant me to be cleansed of all my sins by this water, so that I may appear innocent before Thee *Amen.*

We speak in the following of this preparation, preparation for the hour of the *Sanctum Regum.*

It is necessary to have a knife or penknife, and a new steel lancet or chisel, on the day and hour of Jupiter, on a waxing Moon, than on it, and being finished, you will say on it the following Orison or Conjuration, which will also be used for the knife, penknife and lancet.

Conjuration.

I CONJURE thee, form of Instrument N., by God the Father Almighty, by the virtues of Heaven and by the predominant Stars, by the virtue of the Elements, stones and herbs, and of all the animals; by the virtue of the hail and storms, that thou receive such a virtue; that through thee we may obtain perfection of all things, from which we want to achieve, and that we do pretend to do without harm, without deception, by God the creator of the Sun of Angels. *Amen.*

We recite on it the Seven Psalms, and the following words:

Dalmaley, Lameck, Cadat, Panola, Velous, Merroé, Lamideck, Caldulech, Anereton, Mitraton, Angels most pure, be the guardians of these instruments, they are needed for many things.

Of the Knife.

ON the day and hour of Mars, on the waxing Moon, you will have made a new steel knife, of the size to be able to cut the neck of a kid with a single blow, and you will make a wooden handle on the same day and hour as above; and with the burin you will engrave on the said handle the following characters; then sprinkle and fumigate it, and use it when needed.

$$ \mathcal{G}2\mathfrak{Z}\mathfrak{Z} $$

Manner of Aspersion & fumigation.

Orison to be said while sprinkling.

IN the name of the immortal God, may God sprinkle you N. and clean you of all deceit and all wickedness, and you will be whiter than snow. *Amen.*

Then pour some holy water, saying:

In the name of the Father † and of the Son † and of the Holy Ghost † *Amen.*

This aspersion will serve for every necessary item; so as the fumigation which follows.

To fumigate, it is necessary to have a crucible or melting-pot, in which you place coal newly kindled with a new fire, and let it be well ablaze. On this you will place aromatics, and will fumigate what you wish, saying the following.

Invocation to be said while fumigating.

ANGELS of God, be to our aid, and through you may our work be accomplished. Zazay, Salmay, Dalmay, Angerecton, Ledrion, Amisor, Euchey, Or ; great Angels. Adonay be here and bestow N. the virtue to receive such a form, that by this let our work is accomplished. In the name of the Father † and of the Son † and of the Holy Spirit. † *Amen.*

Recite over it the Seven Psalms, which come after the two *Judicium tuum regida, et Laudate Dominum omnes gentes.*

Of the Skin or Virgin Parchment.

THE virgin parchment is made in several ways. Commonly it is made from the skin of a lamb or kid, or other animal, which must be virgin. After that you will sprinkle it and engrave AGLA on the blade with the burin, after having fumigated it. That if you cannot do this, you will buy a new blade and conjure it, sprinkle it and fumigate it three times. The knife will be used for all your cutting needs, to cut your wands, and for anything necessary. Remember that when the sacrifice is made for the virgin parchment, all the instruments must generally be on the altar; you will make a rod of Elderberry that has never been worn, and you will cut it with a single blow on the day and hour of Mercury, at the crescent of the Moon, and you will engrave it with the burin, the feather or the lancet of the art, with the following characters:

You will make another staff of Hazel wood, which has never borne, and which is without seeds, and you will cut it on the day and hour of the Sun, on which you will engrave these other characters:

This being done, you will say on the staff the following Orison.

Orison.

MOST wise, most powerful Adonay, deign to bless, sanctify and conserve this staff or rod, so that it may have the necessary virtue through you, whose name lives forever and ever. *Amen.*

Then sprinkle and fumigate the locks of the chests.

Of the Lancet.

IT is necessary to have a new lancet, conjured and prepared like the knife and burin. You will make it in the day and hour of Mercury, on the crescent of the Moon, in the following manner.

You will take your Goat and place it on a plate, so that it turns its neck upwards, to make it easier for you to cut it. Take your knife and cut its neck with a single stroke, while pronouncing the name of the Spirit that you wish to invoke. For example, you will say: *I kill you* N. *in the name and honour of* N.

This must be understood in everything you generally do, and remember it well, and take care not to give two blows, but that it dies with the very first; you will then skin it with the knife, and while skinning it, say the following invocation.

Invocation.

ADONAY, Dalmay, Lauday, Tetragrammaton, Ancreton, Areton, and you Holy Angels of God, be here, and deign to give virtue to this parchment, so that it may be correctly preserved, so that all that is written upon it may become perfected.

After it is skinned, take some well-ground salt, then spread this skin, and throw your salt on it, making sure it covers the whole skin; but first you must have the salt blessed as follows.

Exorcism of the Salt.

I EXORCISE you, creature of the Salt, by the living God, by the God of all Gods, and the Lord of all Lords, that all deceit may leave you, and may you serve us to make the virgin parchment.

Benediction of the Salt.

GOD of Gods, and Lord of Lords, who created everything from nothing, and created salt for human salvation, bless † and sanctify this salt, that I may cause that all things which are in this circle receive the virtue which is necessary to produce the effect we desire. *Amen.*

That finished, place your salty skin remain under the rays of the sun for a day, then have a glazed earthenware vase, around which you will write with the pen and ink of art the following characters:

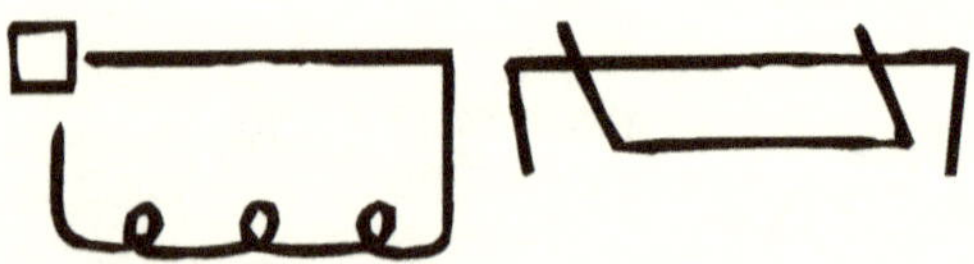

Then put some quicklime and exorcised water into the pot, and while it is liquid, put your goatskin into it, and leave it there until it peels off by itself.

Of the Sprinkling of Water.

LORD God, Father Almighty, my refuge and my life, help me, Holy Father, because I place my hope in you. God of Abraham, God of Isaac, God of Jacob, God of Angels, God of Archangels and Prophets, Creator of all, I most humbly pray to you by the invocation of your Names, although I am unworthy to name them; that you bless and consecrate this water, so that wherever it is poured, it brings back the salvation of our bodies, through you, Most Holy Adonay, whose reign is without end.

After your skin is done, that is to say, the hair will be ready to fall off by itself only by touching it with a finger, take it out of the pot and peel it with a knife made from Hazel wood, on which you will have said the following words:

Most Holy Adonay, put into this wood such a virtue, that it may have the power to cleanse this parchment through your Holy Name Agason. *Amen.*

This being done, the skin being now clean, stretch it on a piece of new wood board, and hold it in place by placing all around it stones gathered from river shores, on which you will say the Orison which follows.

Orison of the Stones.

ADONAY, God very strong and most powerful, grant to these stones that they may extend this skin and remove from it all wickedness, so that by your power it retains the virtue that we desire. *Amen.*

After which, let the skin dry, and before leaving it, say the following Orison.

Orison.

J E, Agla, Jod, Heu, He, Emmanuel, be the guardians of this skin or parchment, so that no phantoms can enter it.

This Orison being finished, leave it in the open air until it is dried.

Nota: that the place must be clean; sprinkle it while saying these holy words.

In the name of the immortal God, may God sprinkle you and cleanse you from all deceit and wickedness, and you will be whiter than snow. *Amen.*

When it is dry, remove it from the wood board and bless it with the fumigation and sprinkling, and keep it for a later use. Take care that it is not seen by women, especially those who have their purges, because it would lose its virtue. The operator who makes this parchment must be very pure, clean and chaste; you will have him say a Mass of the Nativity on the same day of the Feast or another day. Note that all other instruments must generally be present on the Altar.

Of the Aspersion.

YOU will make an aspersorium with mint, marjoram and rosemary. You will tie it with thread that was spun by a virgin maiden; you will use it in all your operations. It must be done on the day and hour of Mercury, the Moon being in its crescent.

Of the Perfumes.

YOU must use wood of Aloes, Incense and Mace. As for the Mace, it is only necessary to perfume the circle, and we will use the other two on all other occasions, on which perfumes you will say the following Orison.

Orison of the aromatic Perfumes.

GOD of Abraham, God of Isaac, God of Jacob, God of our fathers, bless this parchment and increase the strength of its odours, so that it receives in itself the virtue of attracting the Spirits that I will invoke, and let all deceit be cast out of it through you † Most Holy Prince Adonay, who reigns without end. *Amen.*

Benediction of the Aromatic perfumes and odours.

DEIGN, O Lord, to bless and sanctify this odorous creature, so that it may be a salutary remedy for us, that it may bring salvation to our bodies and our souls through your help, Lord Adonay, God who reigns through the infinite centuries. *Amen.*

Of the Quill of the Art.

YOU will have a new feather which you will sprinkle and fumigate like the other instruments, and when you trim it, say the following words, holding it in your hand:

Ababaloy, Samoy, Escavor, Adonay. I have removed all deceit from this quill so that it may hold within with effectiveness the power needed for all those things which are used in this Art, for both the operations, characters and conjurations. *Amen.*

Of the Cornet for the Ink.

YOU will buy a cornet or writing case on the day and hour of Mercury. At the same time, you will write all around the names of God which follows: Jod, He, Va, Hemitreton, Jod, Cados, Eloym,

Sabaoth. Then place your new ink there, after having exorcised it as follows.

Exorcism of the Ink.

I EXORCISE you, creature of Ink, by Anston, Cerreton, Stimulator, Adonay, and by the name of Him who with a single word created everything and can do everything, so that you assist me in my work, and that by my desire may my work be accomplished and brought to a successful end, by the permission of God who reigns without end throughout all centuries. *Amen.*

Blessing of the Ink.

L ORD God Almighty, who governs all creatures, who reign throughout eternity, and who does wonderful things on creatures, give us the grace of your Holy Spirit by means of this Ink. Bless it † sanctify it † and impart it with a very special power, so that everything that we may say, do or desire to write with it, may be accomplished through you, Most Holy Prince Adonay. *Amen.*

Then sprinkle, fumigate and exorcise. He who wants to operate must observe that when all things have been properly prepared without omitting anything, he must also prepare himself in the following manner. He must fast for three days very austerely; let him flee, as much as he can, from the company of others and human conversations, particularly women; that he be withdrawn, and that every morning, when he gets up, he washes his hands and face, pronouncing the following Orison.

Preparatory Orison.

LORD God Adonay, who from nothing formed man in your own image and likeness; it is I, unworthy sinner as I am, who pray to you that you deign to bless and sanctify this water, so that it may be beneficial to my body and my soul, and that all wickedness may come out of me. Lord God all-powerful and ineffable, who brought your people out of the land of Ægypt and brought them across the Red Sea on dry ground, grant me, by this water, to be cleansed of all my sins, so that I may appear innocent before you. *Amen.*

NOTICE.

THIS water must be of that which is exorcised where you put your quicklime. Then you will wipe your hands and face with a clean white cloth, and know and remember that it is necessary and very important to abstain for three days from sin, and especially mortally, as much as human frailty can, and mainly keep chaste. During the three days, apply yourself to the study of the book, because it is certain that if you take especial care, you will understand it easily, although I have not explained it in words expressly, so that it does not become vulgar; because daisies are not for swine; but for those who know how to save their souls, as well as of their body, and always be secretive not reveal it to anyone, lest it become your own fall. Thus, to achieve this, you have to read and reread until you understand it; because it must be enough for you when I tell you that it was on purpose that I did not want to explain it, and that is enough that everything is contained within this work. Dedicate yourself to the invocations, lest you lack memory at the moment of the operation, and that you have committed it by practice, by reciting the following Orison several times each day. Once at Prime, twice at the hour of Terce, three times at the hour of Sext, four times at the hour of Nones, five times at the hour of Vespers, and six times before going to bed. It should be noted that these hours are planetary and unequal. Prime is taken at sunrise; Terce three hours later; Sext at midday; Nones at three quarters of the day, and Vespers at the end of the day, that is why we must settle on this.

Orison.

ASTRACHIOS, Asach, Asarca, Abedumabal, Silat, Anabotas, Jesubilin, Scingin, Géneon, Domol, Lord God, who art in the Heavens, and who looks upon the depths, I pray you to grant me the power, to conceive in my spirit and to execute what I desire to do, and which I want to achieve through your assistance, Almighty God, who lives and reigns throughout all centuries. *Amen.*

All this being done, all that remains is to perform your invocations and trace your characters, and for this purpose you will do as follows.

On the day and hour of Mars, the Moon being in its crescent, and the first

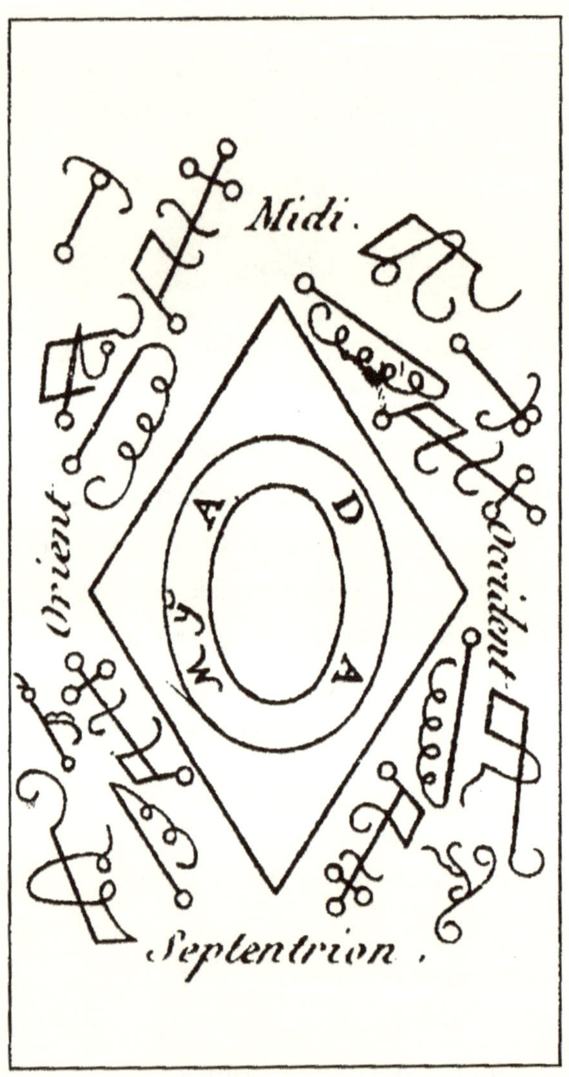

Midi.
Orient
Occident.
Septentrion.
ADAM

hour of the day, which is a quarter of an hour before sunrise, you will prepare a piece of virgin parchment, which shall contain all the characters and the invocations of the Spirits you wish to invoke. For example, on the said day and hour, you will tie your little finger of the hand, which is the finger of Mercury, with thread spun by a virgin maiden, and you will prick your finger with the lancet of the Art to draw blood with which you will form your Scyrlin characters, as it is given here in this work, then write over his invocation, which is the one that follows.

Invocation to Scyrlin.

HELON † Taul † Varf † Pan † Heon † Homonoreum † Clemialh † Serugeath † Agla † Tetragrammaton † Casoly.

See his circle and his character above.

You must write the first letter of your name where is the letter A, and that of your surname where is the letter D, which is the Spirit Aglassis to whom the character belongs, being very swift to be at your service, and makes you have power over the other Spirits. That being done and said, make above the character of the Spirit that you wish to conjure, and burn some incense in his honour. Then write the conjuration which is addressed to the Spirit that you want to cause to appear, and burn incense in his honour.

Conjuration to Lucifer.

LUCIFER † Ouyar † Chameron † Aliseon † Mandousin † Premy † Oriet † Naydrus † Esmony † Eparinesont † Estiot † Dumosson † Danochar † Casmiel † Hayras † Fabelleronthon † Sodirno † Peatham † *Venite* Lucifer. † *Amen.*

Conjuration to Beelzebuth.

BEELZEBUTH † Lucifer † Madilon † Solymo † Saroy † Theu † Ameclo † Segrael † Praredun † Adricanorom † Martiro † Timo † Cameron † Phorsy † Metosite † Prumosy Dumaso † Elivisa † Alphrois † Fubentroty † *Venite* Béelzébuth. *Amen.*

Conjuration to Astaroth.

ASTAROTH † Ador † Cameso † Valuerituf † Mareso † Lodir † Cadomir † Aluiel † Calniso † Tely † Pleorim † Viordy † Cureviorbas † Cameron † Vesturiel † Vulnavij † Benez † meus Calmiron † Noard † Nisa Chenibranbo Calevodium † Brazo † Tabrasol † *Venite* † Astaroth. † *Amen.*

After having said the conjuration seven times, which is addressed to one of the superior Spirits, he will immediately appear to you to do whatever you desire.

Nota. That one must write such a conjuration on virgin paper or parchment before invoking the Spirits; and being satisfied, you will dismiss them, by saying to them what follows.

Dismissal of the Spirit.

ITE *in pace ad loca vestra & pax sit inter vos redituri ad mecum vos invocavero, in nomine Patris* † *& Filii* † *& Spiritus sancti.* † *Amen.*

Conjuration to the Inferior Spirits.

O SURMY † Delmusan † Atalsloym † Charusihoa † Melany † Liamintho † Colehon † Paron † Madoin † Merloy † Bulerator † Donmeo † Hone † Peloym † Ibasil † Meon † Alymdrictels † Person † Crisolsay † Lemon Sesle Nidar Horiel Peunt † Halmon † Asophiel † Ilnostreon † Baniel † Vermias † Eslevor † Noelma †

Dorsamot † Lhavala † Omot † Frangam † Beldor † Dragin † *Venite,* N. †

Instead of the letter N, you will put the name of the Spirit you want to summon. He will appear to you and grant you what you want after which you will send him back with the following words.

Dismissal.

GO in peace, N., to where you come from; may peace be with you, and may you come whenever I shall call you. In the name of the Father † and of the Son † and of the Holy Spirit. † *Amen.*

You have to burn both characters, because they are only used once.

Another Conjuration.

I CONJURE you, N., by the Great Living God, Sovereign Creator of all things, that you appear in a human, beautiful and pleasant form, without noise and without fear, to answer truthfully to all the questions I shall ask. I conjure you by the virtue of these Holy and Sacred Names.

Orison of the Salamanders.

IMMORTAL, eternal, ineffable and uncreated Father of all things I who are borne upon the incessantly rolling chariot of Worlds which are always turning; Ruler of the ethereal immensity where the throne of thy power is elevated; from whose height thy dread-inspiring eyes discover all things, and thy exquisite and sacred ears hear all; Listen to thy children whom thou hast loved from the beginning of the ages; for thy golden, great, and eternal majesty is resplendent above the world and the starry heavens. Thou art raised above them O sparkling fire! There thou dost illumine and support thyself by thine own splendor; and there comes forth from thine essence overflowing streams of light which nourish thine infinite spirit. That infinite spirit nourishes all things, and renders this inexhaustible treasure of substance always ready for the generation which fashions it and which receives in itself the forms with which thou hast impregnated it from the beginning. From this spirit those most holy kings who surround thy throne, and who compose thy court, derive their origin. O Father Universal! Only One! O Father of blessed mortals and immortals! Thou hast specially created powers who are marvellously like thine eternal thought and adorable essence. Thou hast established them superior to the angels who announce to the world thy wishes. Finally, thou hast created us in the third rank in our elementary empire. There our continual employment is to praise thee and adore thy wishes. There we incessantly burn with the desire of possessing thee, O Father! O Mother! the most tender

of all mothers! O admirable archetype
of maternity and pure love! O Son, the
flower of sons! O Form of all forms;
soul, spirit, harmony and number of all
things. *Amen.*

Of the Pentacles or the three Rings
of Solomon, son of David.

I WANTED to put here the figure and
form of the Pentacle of Solomon, so
that you may take the arrangements, they
being of great importance to us.

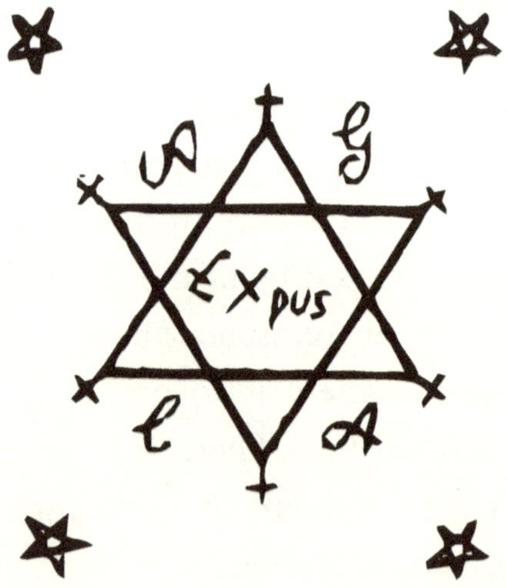

Process.

W HEN you have made your circle, before entering it, you must perfume it with musk, amber, aloes wood and incense; and for the perfume that you will need during the invocations, it will only be incense.

It is to be observed to always have a fire while you invoke, and when you perfume, it will be in the name of the Spirit you want to summon; as well as every time you put perfume on the fire, say:

I am burning this N. in the name and honour of N.

While invoking, you must hold your invocation in the left hand, and in your right, the elder wand; and the alb and the knife will be at your feet. That being done, you will enter the circle. If you have companions, those who accompany you will hold one in each hand. Being inside, you will trace your circle with the knife of Art. And you will pass your wands one after the other, saying the Fiftieth Psalm, namely, the *Miserere mei.*

When the circle is complete, perfume and sprinkle it with holy water. After having traced the characters in the four corners, you must prohibit the Spirits in formal terms from entering inside. After which you will begin your invocations, which you will repeat seven times in a row. And when the Spirit has appeared, you will have him sign the character which you will hold in your hand, with promises to come whenever you call him, and you will ask him what you want and everything you deem appropriate. And when you are satisfied, you will send him back as follows, saying:

Ite in pace ad loca vestra & pax sit inter vos redituri ad mecum vos invocavero, in nomine Patris † & Filii † & Spiritus sancti. † Amen.

<hr>

RARE & SURPRISING MAGICAL SECRETS.

*The manner of making
the Mirror of Solomon,
useful for all divinations.*

I N the name of the Lord. So be it. You will see in this mirror all the things you desire. In the name of the Lord who is blessed.

Firstly, you shall abstain from any action of the flesh or thoughts during the time prescribed below.

Secondly, you will perform many good works of piety and mercy.

Thirdly, take a shiny and well-polished plate of fine steel, which is slightly con-cave, and with the blood of a white pigeon, write on the four corners the names of Jehovah, Eloym, Metraton, Adonay, and put the said steel plate in a clean and white cloth. When you see the new Moon in the first hour after the sunset, go to a window, look at the Sky with devotion, and say:

O Eternal! O Eternal King! Ineffable God, who created all things for the love of me, and by occult judgment for the health of man, look at me and my intention, N., your most unworthy servant, and deign to send me your angel Anael on this mirror, who summons, commands and orders his companions and your subjects whom you have made, O Almighty, who have been, who are, and who will be eternally; that in your name they may judge and act in righteousness, to instruct me and show me what I ask of them.

Then throw suitable perfume on burning coals, and while doing so, say: In this, by this, and with this, which I pour before your face, O my God, who is triune and blessed and in the most sublime elevation, who see above the Cherubim and the Seraphim, and who must judge the age by fire, hear me.

Say this three times; and after having said it, blow as many times on the mirror, and say:

Come, Anael, come, and may it be your good pleasure to be with me willingly, in the name of the most powerful † Father, in the name of the most wise † Son, in the name of the most gracious † Holy Spirit. Come, Anael, in the name of the terrible Jehovah, come, Anael, by the virtue of the immortal Elohim, come, Anael, by the arm of the almighty Metraton. Come to me, N. (say your name on the mirror) and command your subjects that through love, joy and peace they make visible unto my eyes the things that are hidden from me. So be it. *Amen.*

After having said and done the above, raise your eyes to the heavens, and say:

Lord Almighty, who causes all things to move as it pleases you, hear my prayer, and may my desire be agreeable to you. Please, O Lord, look at this mirror and bless it, so that Anael, one of your subjects, may dwell thereto with his companions, to satisfy me N., your poor and miserable servant. O God, blessed and exalted of all celestial Spirits, who live and reign in all ages. So be it.

When all has been done, make the sign of the cross on yourself and on the mirror, on the first and subsequent days, for forty-five days in a row, at the end of which Anael will appear in the form of a beautiful child, will greet you and command his companions to obey you.

Note that it does not always take forty-five days to make the mirror, often he will appear on the fourteenth day, depending on the intention, devotion and fervour of the operator. When he appears to you, ask him what you wish, and let him know to appear whenever you call him to grant your requests.

When you wish to see in this mirror and obtain what you desire, it is not necessary to recite all the above-mentioned Orisons, but having perfumed the mirror, say as above: Come, Anael, come, and may it be your good pleasure, &c. until Amen.

To dismiss him, say:

I THANK you, Anael, for coming and fulfilling my request. Go in peace, and come back whenever I call you.

The perfume of Anael is saffron.

Divination by the word of Uriel.

TO succeed in this operation, he one who wants to perform the experiment must observe exactly what follows.

Let him choose a small room or cabinet which has not been visited by impure women for at least nine days. Let this place be well cleansed and consecrated by aspersions and fumigations, as was said above. There will be in the middle of this room a table covered with a white cloth, and on it will be placed the following: a new glass vial, filled with fountain water, gathered a little before the operation; three taper candles of virgin wax, mixed with human fat; a piece of virgin parchment half a foot square; a quill from a raven ready to use; an earthenware cornet with new ink; a small container filled with material to make a fire. The three taper candles will be nailed with a new and large needle, and placed at equal distance, half a foot away, one behind the vial, and the other two placed to the right and the left. While arranging these, you will say the following words:

Gabamiah, Adonay, Agla, *Domine Deus virtutum adjuva nos.*

The virgin parchment must be on the right side of the vial, and the quill and ink on the left. Before beginning the operation, you must close the door and windows, then stir the fire and light the three taper candles. Then the Master of the operation will look fixedly at the vial, bringing his right ear closer, and in a soft voice and as clearly as he can, he will say the following conjuration.

Uriel, Seraph, Josata, Ablati, Agla, Caila, I pray and conjure you by the four words that God spoke with his mouth to his servant Moses: Josata, Ablati, Agla, Caila and by the nine heavens where you dwell, that you have to appear at once visibly in this vial, to uncover the truth that I wish to know without disguise; which having executed, I will dismiss you in peace and benevolence, in the name of the most Holy Adonay.

After this conjuration, we check if anything appears in the vial, and if we see an angel or something else, the Master of the operation will say in an affable tone of voice:

Blessed Spirit, be welcome. I conjure you once again, in the name of the most Holy Adonay, to uncover the truth, &c.

And if for reasons unknown to us, you do not want to be heard, I conjure you, in the name of the most Holy Adonay, that you write the answer on this virgin parchment, between now and tomorrow morning, or at least to reveal it to me tonight while I sleep.

If the Spirit answers to what was asked, you will listen respectfully; but if he does not speak after having repeated the same supplication three times, you will extinguish the tapers, and will leave the room, closing the door behind until the next morning, upon your return. And you will find what you wish written on the virgin parchment, if it has not been revealed to you during the night.

Divination by the egg.

THE operation of the egg serves to find out what will happen to someone present during the experiment. Take an egg from a black hen, laid that day, break it and we extract the germ. You must have a large glass, very thin and clear. Fill it with very clear water and put the germ of the egg in it. This glass must be placed under the sun at midday in summer, and the Master of the operation will recite the orisons and conjurations of the day [as they are found in the Key of Solomon, where we deal extensively with aerial Spirits], and with the index finger, will stir the water in the glass to make the germ turn. Let it rest for a while and look through the glass, without touching it, and you will see what relates to the person for whom this operation is destined; and it should be carried out on a working day, because then the events present themselves through their mundane occupations. If we want to see if a boy or a girl is a virgin, the germ will fall to the bottom; if he is not, it will be as usual.

To see the Spirits which fill the air.

TAKE the brain of a rooster, the powder from the grave of a dead man, that is, earth that touches the coffin, wal-

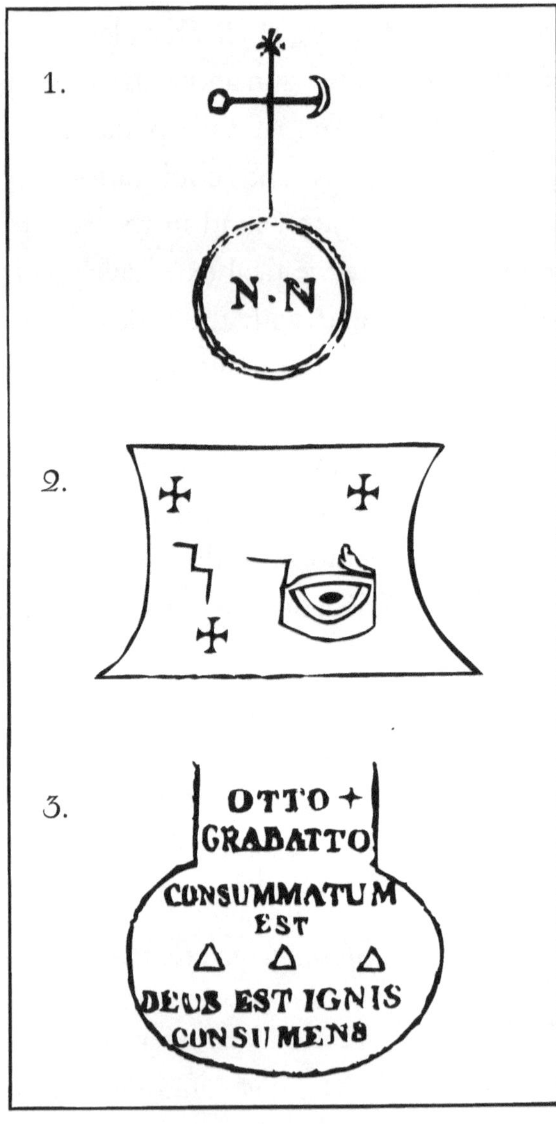

1.
2.
3.
N·N
OTTO +
GRABATTO
CONSUMMATUM
EST
DEUS EST IGNIS
CONSUMENS

nut oil, virgin wax. Make a composition of the whole, which you will wrap in virgin parchment, in which will be written these two words: GOMERT KAILOETH, with the following character:

Burn it all, and you will see prodigious things. But this experiment should be done only by those who fear nothing.

To make three ladies or three gentlemen come in your room, after supper.

Preparation.

FOR three days it is necessary to abstain from drawing Mercury, and you will be elevated. On the fourth day, as soon as it is morning, clean and prepare your room, as soon as you have dressed, all this time fasting, making sure that your room will not be disturbed for the rest of the day.

Note that there shall be nothing hanging or on hooks, like tapestries, clothes, hats, birdcages, curtains, &c. and above all, put clean white sheets on your bed.

Ceremony.

AFTER supper, go secretly to your room, prepared as above. Light a good fire; put a clean white tablecloth on the table, three chairs around, and in front of each place, set a wheat roll and three glasses of clear and fresh water. Then place a chair or seat beside your bed, then go to bed, and say the following words:

Conjuration.

BESTICIRUM *confolatio veni ad me vertu Creon, Creon, Creon, cantor Laudem omnipotentis et non commentur. Star superior carta bient Laudem omviestra principiem da montem et inimicos meos ô prostantis vobis et mihi dantes quo passium fieri sui cisibilis.*

The three persons having arrived, will sit near the fire, drinking, eating and then will thank the one who received them: because if a woman performs this ceremony, three gentlemen will come; and if it is a man, there will come three young ladies. These three people will draw lots among themselves to see who will stay with you: she will sit in the seat or chair that you have provided for them, next to your bed, and she will stay chatting with you until midnight; and at this time, she will go with her companions, without there being any need to send them away. As for the other two, they will stand by the fire while the other talks to you; and while she is with you, you can question her about such art or science, and anything that you wish; she will immediately give you a positive answer. You can also ask her if she knows of any hidden treasure, and she will tell you the place and the convenient time to raise it, and will even be there with her companions to defend you against the attacks of the infernal spirits who could have possession of it; and leaving from you, she will give you a ring, which will make you lucky in gambling by wearing it on your finger; and if you put it on the finger of a woman or young girl, you will enjoy her immediately.

Nota.—That you must leave the window open so that she can come in. You can repeat this same ceremony as often as you wish.

To make a girl come to you, however modest she may be. Experiment of a marvellous power of the superior intelligences.

IT should be observed, from the first quarter to the waning of the moon, a very bright star between eleven and midnight; but before beginning do as follows.

Take a virgin parchment, on which you will write the name of the person whom you desire to come. The parchment must be cut in the manner shown on the first line of the following figure.

The two NN indicates the place for the names. On the other side of the parchment, write these words: MACHIDAEL BARESCHAS; then put the parchment on the earth, the names against the ground, your right foot on it and your left knee on the ground. Holding in the right hand a white wax candle that can last for an hour, look at the brightest star and say the following conjuration.

Conjuration.

I SALUTE thee and conjure thee, O beautiful Moon and beautiful Star, as well as the bright light which I hold in my hand, by the air that is within me, and by the earth that I am touching. I conjure thee, by all the names of the Spirit princes that presides in you, by the ineffable name ON, which created everything, by you, beautiful angel Gabriel with Prince

Mercury, Michael and Melchidael. I conjure thee again, by all the Names of God, that you send to possess, torment, harass the body, the soul and the five senses of N., whose name is written on this parchment, so that she comes to me and fulfills my will, that she has no friendship for anyone in the world, especially for N. as long as she is indifferent towards me. May she cannot endure. May she be obsessed, suffer and tormented. Go, therefore, promptly Melchidael, Bareschas, Zazel, Firiel, Malcha and all those who are under your command. I conjure thee, by the great living God, to send her speedily to satisfy my will. Me N., I promise to satisfy you.

Having repeated this conjuration three times, put the candle on the parchment and let it burn. The next day, take said parchment and put it in your left shoe. You leave it there until the person whom you have made this operation comes to find you. It is necessary, in the conjuration, specify the day you want her to come and she will not be absent.

To put out a fire in a fireplace.

MAKE on the fireplace, with a coal, the characters and words of the above plate, third line, and three times pronounce the words written therein.

To make oneself invisible.

BEGIN this operation on a Wednesday, before sunrise, being provided with seven black beans, then we take a human skull. Put a bean in the mouth, two others in the nostrils, two others in the eyes, and

two in the ears. Next, make on this head the character here shown, then bury the said head with the face towards the sky.

Water it for nine days with excellent brandy, in the morning when the sun is up. On the eighth day, you will find the deferred Spirit there, who will ask you, "What are you doing there?" You will answer him, "I am watering my plant." He will tell you, "Give me this bottle, I will water it myself." You will tell him that you do not want to. He will ask you again, but you must continue to refuse until he stretches out his hand, and there you will see in it the figure similar to the one you made on the head, which will hang from the tips of his fingers. In this case, you must be assured that it is indeed the true Spirit of the head: because someone else could surprise you, causing harm to you and your operation would become unsuccessful. When you have given your flask, he will water it himself and you will take you leave. The next day, which is the ninth day, you will return there; you will find your ripe beans. You will take them; you will put one in your mouth, then you will look in a mirror; if you don't see yourself, it will be good. You will do the same to all the others; or testing them in the mouth of a child. All those which will be worth nothing must be buried where the head is.

To have Gold and Silver, or the Hand of Glory.

PULL out the hair, with its root, from a mare in heat, closest to the nature, saying: Dragne, Dragne, Dragne.

Secure the hair, and immediately buy a new earth pot with the cover, without haggling. Return home; fill this pot with water from a spring, up to two fingers near the edge. Place the said hair into the pot, which you must cover. Put it in a place where it cannot be seen by either you or others, because there would be danger.

1.

2.

3.

After a period of nine days, and at the same time that you hid it, go uncover it; you will discover inside a small animal in the shape of a snake. He will stand upright; you will tell him immediately, "I accept the pact." This done, you will take it without touching it with your hand; you will put it in a new box bought expressly for the purpose without haggling: you will put wheat bran in it, nothing else; but you must not fail to give it to him every day; and when you want to have silver or gold, you will put in the box as much as you want to have, and you will lie down on your bed, putting your box near you, and sleep, if you want, for three or four hours. After this time, you will find double the money you put in; but you must be careful to put the same one back.

Note that the small figure, second line, only comes by the force of the charm; so you cannot put more than 100 pounds at a time. But if, however, your planet gives you dominance over supernatural things, the serpent will be in the likeness of the second figure of the same line as above; that is to say, he will have a face approaching the human face, and you will be able to put up to 1000 pounds; every day you will get twice as much. If we wanted to get rid of it, we can give it to whoever we want, provided that they accept it, putting the figure we have with a cross, to the line made on virgin parchment in the box, or, instead of the ordinary wheat that is commonly given, you will have to give him bran from the flour from which a Priest will have said his first Mass, and he will die; above all, do not forget any circumstance, because there is no mockery in this matter.

Garters for travelling.

LEAVE your house on an empty stomach, walk to your left until you find a merchant selling ribbons. Buy a yard of white one; pay whatever is asked of you, and drop a liard in the shop, return home by the same route. The next day, do the same until you find a merchant selling feathers. Buy one cut, just as you bought the ribbon; and when you are back in your dwelling, write with your own blood on the ribbon, the characters of the third line, it is the white right garter above; those of the fourth are for the left. When this is done, leave your house; on the third day, wear your ribbon and your quill; walk left until you find a pastry chef or a baker; buy a cake or a loaf of bread for two liards; go to the first tavern, order a half bottle of wine, have the glass rinsed three times by the same person, break the cake or bread into three pieces; put the three pieces in the glass with the wine. Take the first piece and toss it under the table, without looking there, saying: "Irly, for you." Then take the second piece and toss it away, saying: "Terly, for you." Write on the other side of the garter the names of these two Spirits with your blood;

2.

N N
MICHAEL +
+ VIRTUS DEU
+
RAPHAEL +
MEDICINA +
+ PARACLETUS +
TETRAGRAMMATON
+ RAGALOT
AGLA +
+ ISCHIROS + ISCHIROS OTHEOS + AGIOS +
+

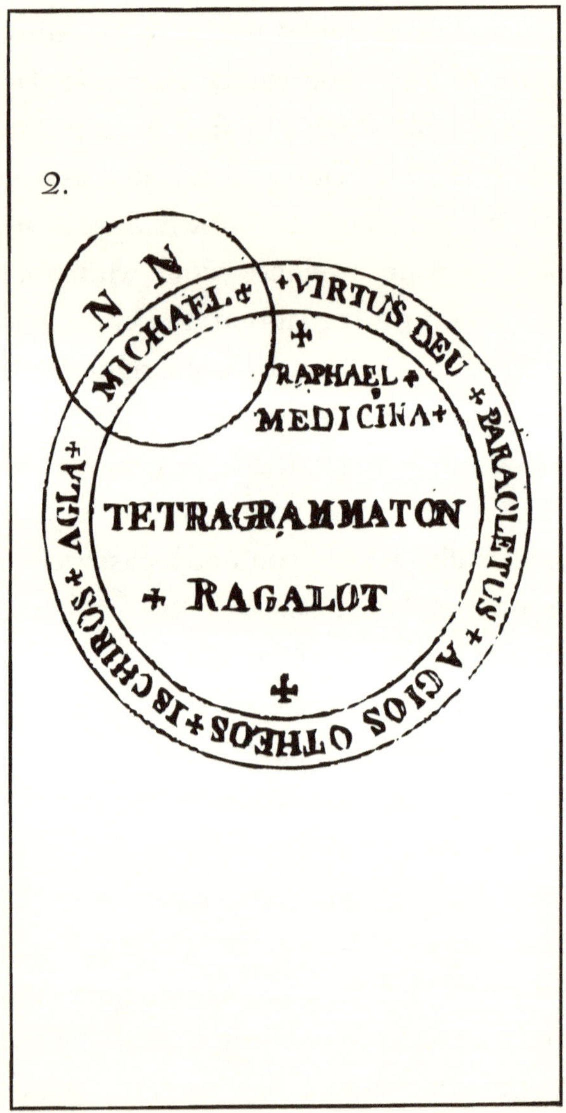

toss away the third piece, saying: "Eirly, for you." Throw away the quill, drink the wine without eating, pay your due and leave. Being out of town, put on your garters; be careful not to mistakenly put the one that is for the right on the left, there is consequence. Stamp your foot three times on the ground, calling out the names of the Spirits: Irly, Terly, Erly, Balthazar, Melchior, Gaspard, let us walk. Then make your journey.

To see at night in a vision, what you wish to know about the past or future.

THE two N.N. which you see in the small circle of the present second figure, shows the place where you must write your name. And to know what you desire, write the names that are in the circle on virgin parchment, being done before sleeping, and put it on your right ear, while retiring, saying the following Orison three times.

Orison.

IN the glorious name of the great living God, to whom, in all times, all things are present to him, I who am your servant N., Eternal Father, I beg you to send me your Angels who are written in this circle, and that they show me what I am curious to know and learn, by Our Saviour Jesus Christ. So be it.

END.

TABLE.

RARE & SURPRISING
MAGICAL SECRETS

www.ingramcontent.com/pod-product-compliance
Lightning Source LLC
La Vergne TN
LVHW041733190726
843493LV00008B/2335